DENISE RENEE DAVIS

God's Beauty For My Ashes

First published by Jadora's Child Publishing 2022

Copyright © 2022 by Denise Renee Davis

All rights reserved. No part of this publication may be reproduced, stored or transmitted in any form or by any means, electronic, mechanical, photocopying, recording, scanning, or otherwise without written permission from the publisher. It is illegal to copy this book, post it to a website, or distribute it by any other means without permission.

Denise Renee Davis asserts the moral right to be identified as the author of this work.

Library of Congress Control Number: 2022909804

This work depicts actual events in the life of the author as truthfully as recollection permits. While all persons within are actual individuals, names and identifying characteristics have been changed to respect their privacy. The author has tried to recreate events, locales and conversations from her memories of them.

Publisher Statement: The author has verified with the publisher that the facts written in this manuscript in this book are true to the best of her knowledge. The publisher will not be held liable for any mistakes, deceptions, fabrications, or any other character defamation. The publisher will not be held liable for the content of this book. The contents of the book and story have been provided by and approved by the author.

First edition

ISBN: 978-1-7346835-4-7

This book was professionally typeset on Reedsy.
Find out more at reedsy.com

This book is dedicated to abused women, men and children. The Dwelling Place Shelter, The Lewis House and Naomi Family Residence Women and Children Domestic Violence Shelter.

Contents

Preface ii
Acknowledgement iii
1 A BEGINNING OF LOVE AND FAMILY 1
2 ABANDONED AND REJECTED 4
3 A TEAR IN THE FABRIC OF INNOCENCE 7
4 BROKEN 12
5 FINDING MY VOICE AND OVERCOMING BULLIES 18
6 STARTING A NEW LIFE 21
7 LOSING THAT WHICH WAS MOST PRECIOUS 34
8 MOVING BACK HOME 40
9 TAKING BACK WHAT'S MINE 42
EPILOGUE 50
About the Author 51

Preface

My name is Denise, and this is my story. I am sharing this story to help someone realize that no matter what you go through in life, God can bring you out. He can teach you how to forgive and move forward free!

When I chose to get healed, I began to realize that my story started way before my life began. I realized that trauma was a theme in my family, and it was as if I was born into it, but I recognize now that it is not where you start (or where your family starts), but where you finish, and I am determined to finish strong. I am determined to be healed.

This story is about the generational trauma that was endured for generations and my determination to get healed. My story is full of trauma, hurt, betrayal, violence, sexual assaults and so much more, but thank God I am free. I no longer have the stains of my past. God freed me from the horror and cycles of abuse, and now I am free.

I am sharing this story now because it's time – time for me to share what was done and how God brought me through, so you will know that He can do this for you.

I pray that my story encourages you, blesses and helps you to know that God is real, and He can give you Beauty for Ashes.

Acknowledgement

I would like to acknowledge those who encouraged me to write this book:

Jasmine Binder, Liela Fuller, Patricia Carter, Maria Davis and Dr. Mary Joe Winston. Thank you for your encouragement.

1

A BEGINNING OF LOVE AND FAMILY

I was born in East Cleveland, Ohio, and my family home consisted of me, my parents, and my two siblings. While I don't remember much about my childhood, there are moments of clarity that have marked my life. When I was little, we did not have everything we wanted, but our family was the picture of love and happiness. Our home was a large single-family home that was warm, welcoming, and inviting. My mother decorated our home with beautiful furniture. She decorated the walls of our home with photos of my siblings and me. Our kitchen was beautiful, and there was always something great l to eat in our home. It had a big porch and backyard, and it was perfect for sitting on the porch talking to my friends and eating ice cream. Sometimes, my friends and I would run through the large attic and play hide and go seek. My home was my haven as a little girl, and I never wanted to be anywhere else.

In the summer, my mom would BBQ on the grill, and she would make potato salad and chocolate cake, which was my favorite. I always loved those days because my mom seemed to love cooking and making us happy. My mother was a heavy-set black woman with soft black hair. She had beautiful brown skin, large lips, and a fat nose. I thought my mom had a nice figure. Even though she had a large stomach and big legs, she was still beautiful to me. She would often wear short knee-length dresses and walk around barefoot. Her hair was always natural, and she seemed to always smell like fried chicken.

Our home was within walking distance of my school, but I dreaded going to school. I didn't like school because the kids teased me. I never wanted to be at school because I felt like an outcast. I didn't have a lot of friends at school. My best friends - Teresa and Renee - lived in my neighborhood, and we did so many things together. Renee was older than me and had a boyfriend, but she still hung out with Teresa and me. Teresa and Renee lived across the street from my house. We would often run up and down the street, racing to find out who was the fastest. I don't remember who won, but I enjoyed every minute of being with my friends. On hot days, we would wait for the ice cream truck to come into our neighborhood, so we could get a cool treat. I would buy the screwdriver ice cream, and they would buy bomb pops and snow cones, and we'd sit in my house and eat them. I loved being with my friends and my family.

My mother was easygoing, and she seemed to always have time for us. She would chase us around with the water hose–it was so much fun to get away from the spray of the hose. We'd laugh and run as fast as we could, but she would always get us. My dad was in the Navy, so he would go away for long periods, but when he came back, he would bring us lots of food and gifts. While I loved seeing my father, his presence often meant fights with my mother.

One Halloween, my dad came in the door, and I thought he was Spider-Man. I was young, and in those days, I thought Spider-Man was real. He came in sneaky like Spider-Man and I said to him, "I thought you were Spider-Man," and he said, "I am!" and he grabbed me and tickled me! It was so much fun! While I was lying on the couch next to my dad, my mom came in screaming at him. I don't remember everything she said, but I know now that it was the beginning of the end. Two short years later, my dad left us for good. At first, I thought he was away in the navy, but days and weeks went by, and he never came home. I would stand by the door waiting for him, but each day that passed without him took more and more of me. By the time I realized he wasn't coming back to us, I felt completely empty inside without him. My dad was my entire world and when he left us, I felt broken.

When my father left us, my mother changed. She went from being a loving mother to something almost unrecognizable. She became a different woman and that set me on a course of pain, destruction, and heartache. My feeble young mind could not comprehend this change. I did not understand why this was happening – it was like something switched in her, and I was helpless to stop it. I tried to understand why she changed, but the only thing I kept coming back to then was the absence of my father. Little did I know there was so much more to the story. I understand that the trauma I dealt with started before I was ever born. It was a generational curse laid long before I was even a thought for my father and mother. The cycle of abuse started years before when my mother was a little girl

2

ABANDONED AND REJECTED

Broken Dreams & Fractured Souls

When my mother was a girl, her family moved to Ohio. My mother's uncle promised my grandmother and her 14 children–including my mom - a better life in Cleveland. But, once they arrived in Ohio, he took them to the country and left them in a town called Ravenna and left them there. This was not the plan, but my grandmother trusted her brother. When they arrived in Ravenna, my mother was a teenager. When they lived in Ravenna, my mother was sexually assaulted by her brother. Unfortunately, this was not the first time. Before moving to Ohio, my mother's stepfather molested her. I don't know how long the abuse lasted, but I know that my mother was not even a teenager yet. My mother would often run to her grandmother's house to be in a place of safety and escape the abuse of her stepfather. My mother moved in with her grandmother to avoid the abuse. Even after she moved, her stepfather would try to get her to come back, so he could continue to abuse her.

My mother saw countless cycles of abuse. From her own molestation and rape to watching her grandmother's husband beat her. My mother suffered through and saw so much abuse that I think she somehow thought it was normal. I can't help but think this abuse shaped my mother's life, and ultimately my own.

While they lived in Ravenna, my mother, grandmother, and my mother's siblings lived in poverty. My mother would often tell me stories of how they would have to eat birds and other wild animals to survive. She said they would often beg their neighbors for food to eat because they had nothing. It was so hard for them, but a year later my mother's uncle made good on his promise to move them to Cleveland.

What happened to my mother shaped how she saw not only the world but our family. My mother saw my father as someone who would help her climb out of the pain of her past, but when he left, she changed. I wanted to believe that this was the hurt and pain talking, but it was not.

Before my dad left us, things with my mom were great. My mom would let us have water balloon fights on hot summer days. My dad made sure we had everything we needed, but when he left, something in my mom changed, and it was not good. At first, I tried to imagine that my dad was on a long-extended vacation, and I would look out the window every chance I got. After months of waiting for him, I got tired of waiting and realized he wasn't coming back, so I stopped looking for him. I felt as if he abandoned me, my mother, and my siblings.

It was as if someone sucked out all the joy, love, and light and replaced it with a gray rain cloud. My aunts would stare at me and tell me I was not my father's child because of my complexion. These people were supposed to love, protect, and support me. Instead of loving me, they degraded me for something I knew nothing about. I was heartbroken. I was a child, but the trauma of their words hurt me almost as much as the abandonment of my father.

After my father left, my mother met a new man, and not long after, she changed. The loving mother who used to play with us became someone who

I barely recognized. She became someone who didn't work and didn't have healthy boundaries. It was as if she'd turned into Dr. Jekyll and Mr. Hyde. I often went to bed wondering if she would have become this person if my dad were still around. There was no way for me to know. I just had to endure the pain of who she had become, and it was painful.

My mother's new relationship coupled with my father's absence ate at the fabric of what was once our happy life.

Love Changes

After my dad left, everything changed. My mom's new relationship intensified who she was becoming. He brought out the absolute worst in her, and I hated him for it. She became distant with us – her children – and even though we needed her, she seemed to need him more. There was no more playing with us in the yard, no more eating good food and enjoying family time. In fact, most days we didn't eat at all because this new man took my mom's food stamps. When we asked my mom about food, she would tell us to eat at school because there was no food in the house. I don't know what her man was doing with my mom's food stamps, but I knew I was hungry and so were my siblings. I would be so hungry some days, that I would beg our neighbors for food just so I could eat something. My mom didn't seem to care that we were hungry or needed her love and attention. She even stopped hugging us and spending time with us. Before my dad left, everyone loved my mom, especially us, but she was no longer lovable and no longer cared. As I look back on it now, she didn't have healthy boundaries. I wonder if the pain of my mom's past causes her to shut down when confronted with her life without my father. I wasn't sure, but I wanted my mom back.

3

A TEAR IN THE FABRIC OF INNOCENCE

My first memory of being molested was when I was around 7 years old. My grandmother and my mom left me with my cousin, my aunt, and my uncle while they went downtown. While I was there, my uncle tried to play this game with my cousin and me, where he would chase us and expect us to chase him back. This game always ended with him touching us inappropriately. At first, I went along with it, because I didn't know that the outcome would be him invading my innocence.

Every time my mom left us there, I wondered why she would trust him to watch us. Whenever she would leave us with him, I would ask her if I could go with her instead but would ignore me. I was devastated. I didn't tell her what was happening, but I thought if I asked her enough, she would wonder why I didn't want to stay with him. I needed protection, but I didn't get it.

My life was on a downward spiral. Soon we were moving out of our family home and into my grandmother's house, where my uncle stayed. When we moved in with my grandmother, I slept in my grandmother's room. I thought I would be safe with her, but I wasn't. My uncle would wait until everyone was asleep and creep into my grandmother's room.

He would take me out of my grandmother's bed, put me on his shoulder, and carry me up to the attic. I hoped my grandmother would wake up and catch him, but she didn't. When we got to the attic, my uncle laid me down on the bed with my cousin and aunt and they were all naked in the bed. He took my clothes off too, and he took turns molesting us. I was so terrified that I couldn't even scream as I wanted to. I also could not understand how he was able to molest my aunt and cousin and neither of them said anything. I could only imagine that they were as scared as I was of him and what he might do to us.

I couldn't believe he was bold enough to take me out of my grandmother's bed. He had no fear of getting caught and that scared me. I couldn't believe he could do these terrible things to us and get away with it. I kept hoping that this was a bad dream, and I would soon wake up, but it wasn't. I tried to pretend to be asleep, and I hoped he would just not touch me, but he did. He would rub his penis on me, my aunt, and my cousin while fondling us; it was sick. After he molested me, he picked me up and took me back to my grandmother's bed. I don't even think my grandmother realized I was gone or the horrific things that happened to me. I was heartbroken and I could not believe that something so devastating could happen to me. I hoped and prayed that one day it would all come out and that something would happen to him.

One day, while my cousin was talking to her mother and stepfather. My mother, uncle, aunt, and grandmother were upstairs talking. I overheard them say that someone touched my cousin. I thought for sure they were talking about my uncle, so I blurted out, "Yeah, he did it." They all looked at me, shocked that I would know anything about it, but no one stopped to ask me why I would say such a thing. They all looked at me as if I wasn't supposed to know anything.

My grandmother panicked and took my mom and aunt downstairs to talk to them about what I said. When they came back upstairs, my grandmother made it very clear that she did not want my uncle to go to jail. There was no discussion about my feelings or even my cousin, who was also molested by him. I felt guilty because I exposed the family secret, or at least revealed that my cousin was telling the truth. I felt like every family member in my grandmother's house that day hated me because I told the truth. I couldn't believe it, and I wanted out of my grandmother's home and out of my family. Thankfully, God delivered me from having to live in the same house as my uncle.

Not long after the revelations came forth about my uncle, my mom moved out of my grandmother's house. We didn't move far–next door–but I hoped the distance would be enough to keep my uncle's hands off me. Yet, I was still afraid that somehow my uncle would hurt me for telling on him.

After we moved out of my grandmother's house, I thought things would change and I thought I would be safe. Our home before my dad left was a place of safety and solitude so I hoped that moving into a home with my mom would be safe. Before my dad left, I never had to worry about anything, but when we moved it was different. The house felt like a house of horrors. There was always something scary lurking in the shadows and I was always afraid. The house was infested with mice and roaches, and I was afraid to go to the bathroom at night.

Whenever I would walk into a room, I would see a roach or a mouse and be petrified. At night, if I went into the kitchen and turned on the light the floors and the walls would be flooded with mice and roaches. It was like a rodent takeover, and I hated it. Not only did the house have mice and roaches, but there was also a threat that I hoped I would never have to face again. I thought when we left my grandmother's house, I would be safe with my mom in a home with her, but I wasn't.

After we moved from my grandmother's house, my mom and her boyfriend got married. This man changed her in the worst way; it was like she was a different person. When my dad left, she changed, but she was a person I no longer recognized. She didn't care about the things that went on in my life and she turned a blind eye to what was happening to me.

I used to love being with my mother and spending time in her bed, but when she married again, that changed.

I was forced to be in their bed not to be with my mother, but for his pleasure. He would keep me in their bed, stained with urine and blood. Their bed never seemed to have sheets, pillows, or blankets on it. It was just the hot mattress and me in the middle of them. He seemed to get a thrill from keeping me in the bed with them so he could molest me whenever he felt like it. I am not sure if my mother knew what he was doing, but I figured she had to know because she, too, was in the room.

I went from loving being in my mother's room to hating it. The room was always humid. They kept the window open to let air in, but because there was no screen, mosquitoes would come in and bite me. At night, the window was like a door into a black abyss, and I was terrified of what might come through the door.

My mom's room faced an alley, and I could hear gunshots and people walking through the dark alley late at night. In my mind, it seemed like those horrible things could walk through the window and snatch me away or kill me. As scary as that was, some days dying or taken seemed better than what was happening in my mother's bed.

Her husband started molesting me when I was 8 years old. At first, it was him rubbing my legs, but soon he was looking at me like I was his girlfriend, and it made me so uncomfortable. I couldn't understand why he was looking at me that way.

One day, while he was sitting at the bar in our house, and he called me over to him. He started singing the song, "You are my lady," by Lionel Richie. He was singing it to me and because it was my favorite song, I started singing too. I soon realized that he was looking at me the way he would look at my mom, and I didn't know what to do, so I ran outside.

I wanted my mother would say something to him about the way he was looking at me, but she never did. Whenever she'd see him looking at me that way, she would put her head down and walk away. I needed her to say something, but she was always silent. She allowed this to happen to me, and I was so angry at her.

He continued to get close to me, and he continued to molest me. My mom didn't say anything about him treating me as if I was his other woman. He would buy me things and not my siblings, and I didn't understand why. He was grooming me. I often wonder what hold he had over my mother because he didn't seem to hide his attraction to me. I often wondered who would protect me because I did not feel safe anywhere.

4

BROKEN

As things progressed at my mother's house, I felt trapped. I wanted to feel safe at home, but I didn't. All I wanted to do was be a kid and enjoy kid things like everyone else in my neighborhood. The only solace I had was riding my bike in the neighborhood. Even though the bike was a gift from my mother's husband, it still represented freedom for me. I always wanted a bike, but it was something my mother could never afford, so he brought it for me. I hated that it came from him, but riding my bike gave me a much-needed taste of freedom from him and my mother.

I would ride my bike all over town and it was so much fun. One day, I rode my bike over to my cousin's house and her neighbor stole my bike. I was devastated! I knew who took it, but the girl never admitted to it. It was obvious to me they stole it, and they had no remorse. I didn't know how to get my bike back. I knew that my mom and her husband wouldn't help me if I told them, so I was on my own. Not to mention, I still had to get back home. These girls had no idea that when they stole my bike, they were also stealing my freedom. I knew that now I would have no choice but to be at home with my mom and her husband. All I could do was cry and walk back home.

Now that I had no way to get around, I had to face my mom and her husband. I could feel the negative energy from them, but I had to survive. I couldn't run to my grandmother because I knew she wouldn't protect me. It felt like I had no one to turn to because everyone wanted to take advantage of me. I wanted to escape the sexual and mental abuse I was experiencing, but I didn't know how to escape.

When I was in the 5th grade, a lady came into our class and said something to my teacher. After speaking with my teacher, she asked the class if anyone needed to talk. I was pretending like I didn't need help, but I did. I raised my hand and told her that I had nightmares. She took me into a small space, I believe it was our coat closet, and I asked her if she could keep a secret. She said yes and the floodgates of secrets flowed from my mouth. I told her that my mother's boyfriend molested me and after I revealed that, the woman stopped talking to me. I don't know what happened next, but when I got home from school my mom's husband was gone for good. I thought I was finally free. All the abuse and molestation I experienced at his hand was finally over and I was relieved, but I still had scars.

I was so happy that I started singing, "yes, Jesus loves me this I know for the bible tells me so." I was singing it repeatedly in my head because I was so happy. At some point, I began to space out and dissociate, but I didn't care. I finally felt like a child again. I was so happy to be able to sleep in my own room and not be assaulted by him. As I sat on my bed, I looked up and saw a letter sitting on my dresser. When I opened it, I saw that it was from my mother to her husband. As I read the letter, I wondered if she left it there so that I would know she was angry with him for what he did to me.

In the letter, she was cursing him out calling him all kinds of bad words. The letter went on to say that she was going to cut his penis off for touching me. When I finished reading the letter, I put it back on the dresser and didn't say anything. I still wondered if my mother was involved or if she wrote the letter and put it in my room so that I would feel bad for her. Reading the letter should've squashed those thoughts but it didn't. I remember the nights I was forced to be in her bed and while he was having sex with my mom, he was also molesting me. As much as I didn't want to believe my mom knew or participated in my pain, I believed she did.

Not long after I found that letter in my room, my mom's husband was in a car accident. He had a heart attack and died. I wanted justice, and this did not seem like justice to me. I wanted to see his face when the police took him to jail. I wanted to be able to testify and confront him in court. I was bitter and angry. This was not the justice I wanted, but I was still thankful that he could no longer hurt me.

I don't hold any grudges against the family members who molested me. I know now that there was a spirit of perversion attached to them. I forgave my uncle because I realized the spirit of perversion was on him. While that spirit transferred to us when he molested us, I chose not to allow this perversion to continue. I chose to break the cycle of molestation and perversion.

After my mom's husband died, I thought I was free to be a child, finally. I was relieved that I would finally be free. I felt like I could finally start my life over, but I soon became a target for child molesters in my neighborhood. I don't know how I attracted these men, but one after the other I found myself ensnared in the web of abusive men.

It started when I was in my early teens. A man I knew from the neighborhood came up to the side of my house and took me down to the basement. I was not interested in him sexually and I thought he was a friend, which is why I went into the basement with him. But while we were in the basement, he tried to rape me. I froze with fear and could not say no to him, but thankfully he could not penetrate me. For the longest time, I could not figure out why I could not say no to him. I didn't want him, but my lips didn't move to say no and if he had finished, he would've raped me.

When I was 13, I was in my favorite park having a picnic and eating the berries that grew on the trees. I'm not sure if I could eat those types of berries, but I ate them anyway because I was hungry. A man I knew from the neighborhood approached me and before I knew it, he told me he wanted to have sex with me. I found myself in the same situation again and I couldn't say no to him. Up to this point, I never actually had sex so I couldn't even tell you if he penetrated me, but that was his intention. I thought he was ugly and mentally challenged, but I still couldn't say no to him.

When I told his family what he tried to do, they told me how sorry they were and vowed that it would never happen again. I hoped that it wouldn't. I wondered if there was something men could smell on me that made them try to rape me. I wasn't sure what it was I just knew that I wanted to be a child who felt safe in her home and in her neighborhood.

By the time I was 14, I was being noticed again, but this time by our landlord. He would come to the house and pretend to fix things so that he could be close to me. I still found him attractive even though he was in his 20s and married. He and his wife lived upstairs. When he'd come over, he would take me into the bathroom and kiss me. I liked kissing him because I really liked him. With him, I didn't want to say no, even though I knew it was wrong. Deep down I wanted to be loved, and this man seemed to love me.

After a while, it was all too much. I didn't feel the freedom I expected to feel when my mom's husband died. Now, I was going from one man to another it seemed, whether I wanted to or not. It was all too much, and I was ready to escape. I thought leaving Ohio would be the best thing for me, so I decided to start fresh in a new place with new opportunities. I decided to move to Mississippi for a new beginning.

My aunt lived in Mississippi, and she agreed to let me move in with her. I thought she would be able to protect and love me, but I was wrong. seemed like she could protect and love me, but I was wrong. My aunt treated me like a dog, and I felt worse than I did in Ohio. She would call me names like wide nose and every day she would talk about my grandmother. She would talk about the land that she and my grandma shared, and I could tell she was angry about it, but I had no idea why. I found out later that the house that my aunt lived in belonged to my grandmother. I believe that is why she treated me the way she did. My aunt saw me as a threat and a spy for my grandmother, but that's not why I was there. I just wanted to get away from the abuse I endured at home in Ohio.

Unfortunately, being with my aunt was just as bad, if not worse, than being with my mom. My aunt was strict and demanding. I could not shower regularly and even on the hottest day; she wouldn't let me turn on the fan. If I turned on the water, the blow dryer, a fan, or even a light she would tell me to go outside. I did my homework outside because I couldn't turn on any lights. She would say, "you can't pay a penny on my bill." I would try to sneak and turn on the water, but she would hear it running and yell at me to turn it off.

I hated living with her more than I hated living with my mom. My clothes were always dirty, and I hated going anywhere. I always felt as if I was walking on eggshells around her house, and I regretted ever moving to Mississippi.

The only time I wanted to be in Mississippi was when I was with my boyfriend Bay Bay. When I first met him, I was uncomfortable talking to him because he was older than me, but it was clear we had chemistry. I couldn't resist him and as we got to know each other he treated me like a queen. I wanted to be with him all the time and often wondered if he could be my husband. Unfortunately, the problems at my aunt's house grew unbearable. My aunt was verbally and mentally abusive to me. She would put me down and make me feel less than. My aunt would tell me that I was too thin and that I should eat more. Eating wasn't the problem – I just couldn't gain weight like she thought I should. I finally had enough and despite the love of my life being in Mississippi, I moved back home to Cleveland.

I returned to Cleveland when I was around 15. I was hopeful that life would be better, but not long after moving back I was sexually assaulted.

Men in the community pretended to like me, but their goal was to abuse me. They would try to lure me off and rape me. One time, a man pointed a gun at my head to force me to have sex with him, but even with this threat I still refused. I felt like I had a target on my back that said I was easy or would give in, but that was not the life I wanted. No matter how hard I tried to be better, it felt like someone always wanted a piece of me they could not have.

One day, I met a man who promised to buy me new shoes if I went to a hotel with him. I went with him because at the time my family was so poor, that we couldn't even afford a two-dollar pair of shoes. I needed new shoes, but I didn't realize what he wanted from me to get those shoes. We didn't have what we needed, so I hated being poor. I was always teased at school for being poor, it was horrible. So, when this man told me all I had to do to get new shoes was to go with him to a hotel, I went. I never thought he would rape, me but that's what he did. I laid there on that nasty hotel bed too terrified to scream or fight. I must've been in panic mode – I'm not even sure. I just didn't want him to kill me, so I kept quiet. He didn't even buy me the shoes; I was so hurt and disappointed. All I ever wanted was to be like everyone else, but there was always someone waiting to take advantage of me.

5

FINDING MY VOICE AND OVERCOMING BULLIES

I started Glenville High School in 1983. I was excited to start high school because I thought it would be different from my other schools. Before high school, I was surrounded by bullies in school. They made fun of me because I was poor and didn't have the clothes most of them had. I hoped that high school would be different, and in the beginning it was. I enjoyed school and made new friends. By the time I was in the 10th grade, I had a lot of friends, but when I entered the 11th and 12th grades things changed. My friends – old and new – turned their backs on me, and I was once again the target of bullies.

It was like a switch flipped, and I went from having a lot of friends to being the target of all the girls in my class. They would call me Olive Oil, big lips, skinny butt, and they would always make fun of the way I dressed. I didn't have any fashion sense and these girls' made fun of me because of it. I didn't know how to dress, so when I started getting teased for my clothes, I would ask my mom how I looked. She would always tell me that I looked good, but I didn't, and I would get teased even more. I felt like a fool. My classmates would point at me and laugh as I walked through the hall. At lunchtime, the girls would tease me because of the way I ate my food. I didn't want to eat lunch because of the teasing, but because I didn't eat breakfast, I was hungry and ate anyway. It was either get teased or eat my lunch, and I chose to eat my lunch. As much as their teasing hurt, I didn't know how to speak up for myself but, I was not afraid to fight.

Throughout the 11th grade and well into the 12th grade, my classmates bullied me. The bullying was so bad in the 12th grade that I had freshmen bullying me. I was a senior in high school, and these freshmen were treating me like I was a second-class citizen. Whenever I went into the bathroom, they would call me things like "big lips", and I was devastated. I felt as if I couldn't stand up for myself even though they were freshmen, and I was a senior. On the last day of school, I finally got the courage to confront these bullies. I saw two girls who bullied me go into the bathroom, and I rushed in behind them. I wanted to fight them both at the same time, but they ran inside a stall and wouldn't come out. Even though I didn't fight them that day, I never had any issues with them again, and I didn't even have to touch them.

I hoped that being out of high school and being a mother would change the way people treated me, but that was not the case. I was bullied in my neighborhood, just like I was bullied in high school. My neighbors would stare at me as if I was an alien from space. I am not sure if it was because I was a young mom or if they didn't like me.

There was one girl in the neighborhood who bullied me every time she saw me. If I was walking down the street, she would try to block me from walking down the street. I said nothing. I just let her do it because I didn't know what to say to her. But one day, I had enough of her bullying, and I looked her right in the eyes and gave her a mean look. She never bothered me again, and that taught me I didn't have to take bullying.

After that, I allowed the fighter in me to come out. I became a fighter, not because of bullies, but also because of my family. They seemed to fight all the time. We even fought out in the street. Even though I could fight, I didn't want to, but I was forced to fight. Fighting was how my family handled conflict, and it was how things got resolved, or so we thought. One day, my family made me fight this tall girl because she ran up and hit me. I didn't want to fight her, but my aunt, cousin, uncle, and my friend forced me to fight back. After that, I started fighting anybody, and it didn't matter who it was. After I fought that girl in the street, her family came to our house and harassed me. They even pressed charges against me for hitting their daughter, but I didn't care.

When we went to court, the judge said that I was a menace to society. I told him I was defending myself against these bullies, and I was tired of being passive and getting picked on. The girl and her family dropped the charges. I was free to go with no mark on my record.

The fighter was still there as I got older, but I learned to fight less with my hands and more with my mouth. If you were rude to me, I would cuss you out in a second. I would go from 0 -to 100 in no time at all. If someone at a store was rude to me, I would yell and demand to speak to the manager. I would try my best to get people fired if I even thought they were rude to me. I was a mess, and I knew it, but it was all to protect the brokenness inside of me. I wanted to be better, but I didn't know how, and I didn't have good examples to follow.

6

STARTING A NEW LIFE

While I was still in high school, I started working at Woolworth's in Cleveland so I could make some extra money. While I was working, I met a man named Carlos. Carlos would hang out downtown every day and we started hanging out. He was a good-looking man from the neighborhood, and he always wanted to take me out on a date, so one day I let him. We started dating, and he said he wanted to marry me and have babies with me. I laughed at him because I didn't think I could have children, but before I knew it, I was pregnant. I didn't even think I could get pregnant because while I was with other men, I never got pregnant. Now, here I was, a senior in high school and pregnant. I was so embarrassed. Even though I was pregnant, I still finished high school and give birth to my first child–Maria. After high school, I decided not to go to college so that I could take care of my baby, Maria.

After Maria was born, I was not working and living in poverty. I wanted more for myself and for Maria, so I decided to go to college. I enrolled in Tri-C Community College in Cleveland, Ohio. At first, my major was Nursing, but then I decided I wanted to be an X-Ray technician. I did my best, but I eventually dropped out of college because I didn't have a babysitter and I was overwhelmed.

I struggled on my own. Maria's father, Carlos, didn't claim Maria for many years because he was afraid of paying child support.

When I met Carlos, he wanted to marry me, but I felt like I was too young for him. I remember him asking me if I wanted to make some money. I don't think I understood what that meant at the time, but I fell in love with him. I loved him so much that I would do almost anything he asked me to do. I didn't want to lose him at the time, but something told me I deserved better, so I left him.

He would visit every 3 to 6 months, but his visits were always very brief. I ran into him a couple of times when Maria was an infant after turning 1 year old. He would dodge me and tell people that he didn't know who I was.

One day Maria was around 8 years old, and we saw him at the movies with another woman. Maria was inside the movie theater, peeping at Carlos as he was standing in line. He glanced at us and gave me a look as if he didn't know us. Maria asked me, "is that my daddy?" I said yes, but she didn't run to him. In 2000 and again in 2016, I ran into Carlos, and he asked me to marry him both times. I almost married him, but people warned me that he would be unfaithful. I also thought about the times that he could've asked but didn't or all the times he tried to hide Maria and me. He was not the one for me.

My grandmother told me I should just get on public assistance and raise my children. My grandmother said many negative things about becoming a nurse that I almost chose not to go to school. I enrolled in Tri-C Community College to be an RN, but my grandmother's words never left me. My grandmother said my baby would get molested in daycare. If that was not enough to scare me, she would tell me that I would bring home germs from the hospital. Every time I turned around, she had something to say, which drove me crazy. Not to mention, I had my own insecurities about my ability to be a nurse. I dropped out of school and as my grandmother suggested, I got on welfare and continued to live with my mother.

After a while, my mother decided she no longer wanted me in her house. Every morning, she would slam the paper on the table so I could start looking for an apartment. Eventually, she put me out when I was not moving fast enough for her. I wasn't sure why she wanted me out of her house, but she did.

Thankfully, I didn't have to be out on the streets because my uncle took my baby and me into his home. He had an upstairs apartment available, and he let me stay in the apartment with my baby. I was excited to have my own place, even though my uncle had issues. I hoped this would be an excellent beginning for me and my baby.

Unfortunately, my uncle's drug, and alcohol addiction issues soon came to my door. I had to deal with his drama head-on. One day, he came up to my apartment banging on the door as if he were the police. When I opened the door, he was sweating with no shirt on. He wanted me to get high with him. I declined, but he kept trying until I gave in. When I finally gave in, he wanted to rape me. I couldn't believe another relative was trying to assault me. I could not believe this was happening to me. I wondered if there was some wicked curse on my family, so I called someone I knew I could trust to find out what she knew. What she told me blew me away.

She told me incest was a theme in my family. I didn't even know about it at the time and when I found out, I couldn't believe it. She told me there were accusations that my uncle slept with or had a relationship with his mother. There were also accusations that my uncle had a baby with his cousin. She also told me that my uncle was accused of raping my mother and her sister when they were teenagers. That was the last straw for me. I knew my daughter and I were in danger, and I needed to get out of there. I found an apartment and decided to live away from my family.

Out of the frying pan and into the fire

After moving into my own place, I met a man at a club named Darryl. He was a nice guy at first. We were only together a month when I got pregnant, and he swore that I trapped him, but that was never my intention. When I got pregnant, he was living with me. As soon as he found out I was pregnant, he stopped working and started laying around my house as if he owned it. He was a drunk who sold weed to keep money in his pocket, but that money never seemed to make its way into our home. He wouldn't buy food or pay bills. He was a joke, and I couldn't believe that I settled for him. He even cheated on me while I was pregnant. I was beginning to hate him little by little, but I didn't have the courage to leave. Darryl never paid any bills, and if I was gone, he would play the music so loud that my neighbors would complain.

One day I was walking home, and I could hear him blasting from my house all the way up the street. I didn't see Darryl anywhere, so I went into the house and turned the music down. Out of nowhere, he rushed into the house and started screaming at me. I jumped up on the couch because I was afraid of what he might do to me. I had 2 soda bottles in my pocket for later, and when he lunged at me, I hit him with one of the bottles. He snatched me off the couch and threw me on the floor. He punched me everywhere. I fell on a chair facing a window and nearly flew out of the window because he hit me so hard. Thank God I didn't fall out of the third-story window because I would've been seriously hurt.

After Darryl beat me, he raped me. I was in pain all over my body. I asked him to take me to the doctor, but he refused. He hit me again and raped me again. When I finally did go to the doctor, they told me I had a fractured arm. I should've left then, but I stayed with him. I grew to hate him even though I was carrying his child.

In 1989, my 2nd child - Brittaney - was born. I was very poor. I was on public assistance and received food stamps, but it was not enough for most months. My rent was $200.00, and I was getting a little over that in assistance. Darryl was not helping, and my family was no real support, either. To make ends meet, I would have to sell my food stamps to buy diapers and pay bills. When things were tight, I would beg people for money just to buy diapers. We barely had enough food to eat. I was getting WIC, but the food my children ate was hardly covered by WIC. Even though people suggested I sell my body for money, I refused to stoop that low.

A couple of days after Brittaney was born, my cousins came over to help me. Maria was with my sister and my young cousins while I rested. While I was resting, my cousins and my little sister went to the store with Maria. Somehow while they were at the store, Maria got left behind in the store. Maria tried to follow them and got hit by a car. She was around 3 years old, and the impact caused her little body to fly up into the air. I knew something was wrong. I was not superstitious, but I felt something was wrong. I was still recovering from having Brittaney and was having a hard time even walking. My cousins and my sister ran and told me that Maria got hit by a car. I don't know how I made it across the street because I could barely walk. When I arrived, people were helping Maria and the man who hit her was beside himself. I didn't know what to do. The ambulance came to take Maria to the hospital, but I had to go back and get Brittaney. I tried to walk as fast as I could, but I was in so much pain it hurt to even walk.

There were so many things happening all at once. I had to get someone to watch Brittaney and I had no idea where her father was. I was having a melt down and I could not believe this was happening to my family.

When I arrived at the hospital, the social worker and police questioned me. They wanted to know why Maria was alone and why she was in the street. I was a nervous wreck. I thought they would support me, but they were looking for someone to blame. I thought Maria was going to die and these people were talking to me as if I was an unfit parent. They told me that they could charge me with child endangerment because it was my fault that she got hit by a car. I tried to explain that I had just given birth and Maria was supposed to be with my mother. I had no idea my cousin and sister had taken her to the store. They still treated me like a criminal. I felt so bad that this happened to my child, and I started thinking maybe it was my fault.

When the social worker, the police officer, and the doctor left the room, I prayed like never before, "Our Father, who art in heaven, hallowed be thy name; thy kingdom come; thy will be done on earth as it is in heaven. Give us this day our daily bread and forgive us our trespasses as we forgive those who trespass against us; and lead us not into temptation but deliver us from evil. For thine is the kingdom, the power, and the glory forever, amen."

All of a sudden, they allowed me to see Maria. When I went into the room, Maria couldn't sit up, but my grandmother and some sanctified sisters prayed for her. After they prayed Maria was able to sit up! I couldn't believe it! God did it and my baby was able to walk. She had some complications, but she survived and every day she healed more and more. Despite all the things the police and social workers said, they didn't take me to jail, and I did not lose my children.

Even though Maria was ok, I was still struggling, and Darryl was not helping at all. He was living with me for free and I couldn't confront him because I was afraid of him. I wanted to tell him to pay a bill or buy our child some diapers, but I could not bring myself to do that. His mother would bring diapers for the baby and while I was thankful, we were still struggling.

I decided to go get a job at Burger King. I thought I would finally be able to pay some bills and buy my kids some clothes, but I ended up with a broken arm. Once I broke my arm, I couldn't work, and I had back on welfare to try to make the ends meet.

As much as I wanted to marry Brittaney's father Darryl, I could no longer deal with his abuse. It was clear to me that he would continue to be who he was and probably get worse. The Word of God tells us it's better to marry than to burn and it also tells us that God hates divorce and sin. I knew we were in sin, but I could not justify marrying him, especially with the way he abused me.

After we broke up, he stalked me at my mother's house. He even cut the phone line at my mother's house and then called the police and told them that my mother was selling drugs. Before we knew it, the swat team kicked in my mother's door. They pointed their guns at my children, my mother, sister, and brother. While they had their guns pointed at us, my brother tried to get up and they almost shot him. My brother was mentally challenged and didn't understand what was going on.

The police searched everywhere including pampers I had for my baby. They found a raggedy gun on a scale in my mother's drawer. An undercover cop also claimed she brought drugs from my mother's home. I knew it was all a lie and it was Brittaney's father making this all up. He would not leave me alone and he was mad at my mother because she helped me get away from him.

Not long after we broke up, he started seeing a woman who lived next door to my mom. He would leave the curtains open so I could see them together. They would drink champagne and then they'd go upstairs. I was hurt but I tried my best to ignore them.

After he called the swat team to my mother's house, I knew I could never go back to him. It was clear that he didn't care about me, his child, or my family because we all could have been killed that night. I was heartbroken but, I tried to stay strong for my children as a single mother. I found a job, but I had nobody that I could trust to watch my children. I let my mother keep them, but I couldn't focus on work. I kept thinking about how she didn't protect me, so why would she protect them? As much as I wanted to believe they would be ok, I worried about them when I was at work, which made it hard to focus on my job.

I began to question God, "Why God? Did this happen to me? Why can't I be with Brittaney's father?" I knew deep down that he didn't care for me. Even though he abused me, I still wanted God to work a miracle and fix our relationship. When I knew it was over and that I couldn't be with him anymore, I told him I was leaving and moving to Mississippi. He had the audacity to tell me, "You can't leave me, you love me."

I loved him, but I knew Ohio was no longer what I needed, so I left. I finally dared to let go of the toxic relationship that lasted 3 years.

Nothing was working for me in Cleveland, so I decided to move back to Mississippi to be with Bay Bay. He told me before I left that when I graduated high school, I could come back, and we would get married. I wanted to be his wife because I loved him so much. The last time I saw him was before I moved back to Cleveland, but I hoped the love was still there.

When I got back to Mississippi, I thought I would move right in with him, but he had a girlfriend. He said was confused and unsure if he wanted her or me. I was devastated, so I packed up and moved back to Ohio. I was so hurt because I thought we would finally be together. In my heart, I hoped that he would choose me, but he decided to marry his girlfriend.

By the time I was 22, he separated from his wife, and he started sending me flowers trying to win me back. I was so desperate to be with him that I packed up again and moved back to Mississippi. We were finally together, but his divorce was still not final, so I had to move back in with my aunt. I stayed in Mississippi, hoping that we would get married and start a family once his divorce was final. Before long, I was pregnant with his child, but he was still married. I know we should've waited until the divorce was final, but our love for one another was unstoppable.

It was not the life I expected when I moved back to Mississippi, but I loved him and was willing to do anything to be with him. While I was pregnant

STARTING A NEW LIFE

with his child, I continued to live with my aunt. I thought pregnancy would be good, but I was sick for most of it. I remember my aunt fussing at me because I wouldn't eat or walk. My pregnancy was high-risk, so I needed to eat and walk. Some things my aunt wanted me to eat were not good for me, like half-cooked ribs. I wondered if she really wanted me to even have a healthy baby. I ended up in the hospital because I almost miscarried. The pregnancy took a toll on me, and I wondered if it was because I was trying to be with a man who was still married.

It turns out the pregnancy was not the only reason I was sick. I found out that my aunt was doing voodoo to run me off. When his family found out I was pregnant, they called me a homewrecker, and they told me to go back to Cleveland. I didn't want to leave because I thought we would get married once his divorce was final. After a while, everyone who was against us being together got their wish, and I moved back to Ohio.

~~

In 1992, I moved back to Mississippi to be with Bay Bay and start a new chapter in my life. I was hopeful that it would be better than the last chapters. When I moved back to Mississippi, Bay Bay and the sisters from church tried to help me forgive those who hurt me, but I had a hard time. I didn't think I could forgive my mother, my mother's husband, my uncle, and my ex-boyfriend.

I thought they were trying to force me to forgive so that I would stop talking about what happened to me. So, I told them that I forgave my mother, but I couldn't forget. Many years later I learned that total forgiveness would set me free.

Forgiveness is not approving of what the person did but releasing them from it so you can move on. Jesus wants us to forgive others the same way he forgives us. Forgiveness is not always reconciliation. It took me many years to forgive people who hurt me. I had to learn to surrender my pain and acknowledge what others did to me and release those who hurt me to the Lord.

Eight months after arriving back in Mississippi, I was pregnant again and we got married. Even though two of my children were not by him, Bay Bay treated them like they were his own. I thought we were a picture-perfect family, but not long after I had our daughter, Jasmine, he changed.

He would yell at my daughters and tell them to shut up. He would curse at them and me for no reason. He went from being this kind soul to this mean man I didn't recognize. I felt like I was always walking on eggshells around him. This was not what I moved back to Mississippi for, but I was too in love to leave him. He was always putting me down. He was even verbally abusive. He often said he was only staying for the children because he didn't want to have anything to do with me. I thought about moving back to Cleveland, but I was too embarrassed.

I wanted to make things work, but it was clear he wanted out. I would pray and ask God to save him and save my marriage. I even prayed that God would change my in-laws, but nothing seemed to change. As things got worse, he would say all kinds of crazy things to me about my church, my friends, and even my daughter. I grew tired of his insults and started to hate him because of it.

I would cry and pray to God, "God where are you? Why won't you rescue me, I messed up again. Why do I keep getting mistreated over and over again? I need your help, Lord! Lord, please save my husband and save me, fix my marriage, change the hearts of my in-laws. What is going on Lord? Why is my husband mistreating me? Should I leave or should I stay and take this abuse?"

As I waited for God to answer, I read my bible and I kept praying, but I couldn't hear from the Lord. I didn't believe in divorce. Until death do us apart, I believed in making it work through sickness and health. I prayed for my husband to change, get saved, and sanctified. When he started going to church, I thought it was the answer to my prayers, but he didn't change. As soon as church was over, he would go back to his old ways. He would compare my church with his church. He would call the people at my church a bunch of holy-rollers and he would call us freaks for the way we worshiped. He wouldn't even allow me to take the kids to church with me, they had to go with him.

There was so much confusion in our marriage. We were living in poverty because even though he had a job, times were hard. I wasn't working because I was taking care of the children. I had four kids at the time and since I wasn't working, he would give me an allowance. At first, he would give me $20 a week, then down to $5 a week, then he stopped giving me money altogether.

Instead of giving me the money, he would give the money to his favorite daughter, Denisha. He started treating me like a child. He demanded that the house be spotless because he claimed to be a neat freak. He was trying to control me and the kids that were not his. He would come home from work and my children race to clean up. They would pick up their toys and throw their things in the closet or under the bed. He would come in looking for a crumb piece of paper, anything to accuse me and my girls of not keeping the house clean. I had to wait until he got home before I could cook dinner.

One day he came home and said to me, "I don't feel shit, I swear to god my mama told me the only reason I'm here is for the kids." I would threaten him with child support, and he told me that his sister could help him beat the case. I wanted to leave him, but I knew I couldn't because I was pregnant again.

One day my class ring went missing and I knew he took it. Even though he was supposedly helping me look, he wasn't really helping. I told him I knew he had my ring, but he told me he could do whatever he wanted to do. He said, "whatever I want to do around this camp, I do. I pay all the bills." I realized he pawned my class ring, and I was never going to get it back. The ring had a lot of sentimental value to me, but he didn't care at all.

One day he came home and decided to pick a fight with me. He pushed me around the house then he tried to choke me with our kids watching. The kids tried to help me, but he was too strong for them. The kids later told me that he had his hand around my neck, picked me up in the air, and stepped on my prescription glasses. The kids told me that after he did all this he started laughing. I couldn't believe this was my life. I left him many times, but I kept coming back.

Two wrongs don't make a right...

A few years later I started working at Shoney's and I met a man named Fred and we started seeing each other. I knew it was wrong because I was still married, but I had enough of my husband's abuse and behavior.

I never expected to be in an abusive marriage. When we met years ago, he never mistreated me, and that's why I came back to him repeatedly and why I married him. Now, my husband was mentally and physically abusive toward me. He stopped treating me like a wife. He stopped, holding my hand. He stopped kissing me and hugging was out of the question. When we had sex, he wouldn't face me, he would turn me on my side, so he didn't have to look me in the eye.

I decided I wanted to try counseling to see if it would help because I thought I was the problem. I begged my husband to go with me but refused. When he finally decided he wanted to make it work, I was done. It was too late, and I no longer wanted him. I decided it wasn't going to work out. Part of me wanted to work things out, but in the back of my mind, I didn't think I could ever trust him again.

One day, my daughter said that my husband fondled her and while I wasn't there, I was not sure I could trust him. I wanted to believe my daughter because I knew what it was like when someone did not believe you. The problem was she kept changing her story which did not help our case. When the police investigated, they said they didn't find any signs of molestation. Even though there was no evidence I needed to believe my daughter. I couldn't live with myself if something happened to her, and I stayed. So, my husband and I got a divorce. After all the years of wanting him and hoping we'd be together forever – our marriage was over.

I wanted to keep my children safe from molestation and so many other things, but I failed to protect them. When I realized it happened to them, I stood up and leave, but it was later than it should have been, and I felt guilty. I felt as if I were no better than my abusers. I had to fight the battle in my mind that caused me to have flashbacks of my abuse at the hands of my uncle.

Leaving your abuser doesn't mean you are free. Despite what I went through, I'm a survivor, not a victim. A survivor has overcome the victim's or abuser's identity and lives consistently with healthy boundaries, good communication skills, and stable emotions. My process of overcoming domestic abuse started with my saying yes to the Lord because I needed a savior. I want to be who God says I am, and that means forgiving those who hurt me.

7

LOSING THAT WHICH WAS MOST PRECIOUS

When I divorced my husband, I was still seeing Fred. He didn't seem to mind that I had 5 kids, and I was thankful for that. Fred and I moved to Lorain, Ohio. By now, Maria was in foster care, and I wanted to get her back. Maria ended up in foster care in Cleveland. The courts told me to take her home, but I couldn't handle her. She was out of control! She would fight her siblings and she would not listen. Maria didn't want to go to school, and she kept running away. I even found her in a van with some woman. She was with this woman willingly, but I didn't know the woman and I was so worried about her. When I found her in that van, I tried to yank her out but that turned into a fight. She was tussling and resisting, and I was trying to spank her to get her under control. I know now I was wrong for the way I handled everything, but I wanted my daughter to be safe. As we tussled, she kicked me off of her and the police came. Maria was taken to a detention home and we had to go to court. I just couldn't handle her. When we went to court, I pleaded with them for help, but the courts refused to help me. They told me to either take her home or they would put her in foster care. So, she went to foster care. I was trying to keep it together, but I was so depressed that I ended up on medication for depression.

I tried to get her back, but she was told CPS she didn't want to be with me in Mississippi. The foster mother sent Maria back because she couldn't handle her either. After that, Maria went with her father, and he couldn't handle her either. Maria ended up in a group home and they couldn't handle her. She was going from house to house, and she end up pregnant. She never came back to Mississippi, but she stayed in Ohio.

Not only were there issues at home, but there were issues in the neighborhood, too. One day, there was a fight in our neighborhood. When I opened the door, about 100 girls wanted to fight Brittaney.

Brittaney picked up a lamp and threw it trying to defend herself against these kids. The next day I looked outside, and my daughters were fighting this girl. I was about to go outside when the girl's mother went up to my daughter and hit her. I ran over to the mother because she would not put her hands on my daughter and not get my wrath. She punched me right in the eye and I saw stars. I started pulling her hair and tried to poke her eyes out.

The next thing I know the police were yanking me off of her. It was like the entire neighborhood was against us, so I packed up my family, including Fred, and moved to Atlanta. Not long after we moved to Atlanta, Fred decided he wanted to go back to Mississippi, so I took him back to Mississippi.

Unruly Children

In 2004, I was living in Atlanta Georgia, with 4 of my children. Maria was in foster care, and I was trying to get her out, but she wanted to be adopted.

I started drinking to cope with everything going on in my life. Sometimes I would smoke some weed with my boyfriend, but it wasn't often because it was too strong for me.

My daughters were always fighting with each other and other girls at school. Sometimes they would skip school altogether. They were so unruly. One of them even broke into the school to get revenge on a mean teacher. She trashed the school with milk cartons and tore pictures off the wall. One of my daughters even stabbed a girl in her back In Mississippi. Thank God the young lady survived, and my daughter didn't serve time.

I was trying to work. I had two jobs: no child support and no family support. I didn't have a babysitter. While I was at work, my daughters would skip school and hang out with older men who sold and used drugs. My daughters robbed the dope man and broke into his house. I don't think they realized the number of times they could've been killed. They blamed it on a boy in the neighborhood, but they took part. I had to keep chasing grown men away from my daughters because they were always at my house while I was not there. When I would catch them, I would call the police and ask them to provide me with the identities of these men, but no one would give me that information.

I believed these men were having sex with my Denisha and Jasmine, and I didn't want that for my daughters. Eventually, Jasmine ended up in a group home and one of my other daughters ran away. Brittaney started fighting her sisters, and she missed 45 days in school one year. She was hanging with the wrong crowd. I thought she was affiliated with a gang, and I was so afraid for her.

I was afraid that Brittaney would get pregnant, drop out of school, join a gang, end up in jail, or even get killed. I wanted a better life for her and all my daughters. I wanted them to finish high school and have a better life.

I was always getting calls from the school about my daughters. The school would threaten that if I didn't control my children, I would go to jail. I had to come to hearings at the school and the school monitored my children's attendance. I would have to sign off on the hearing letter that had their school attendance record for that month. If my children were absent over 3 times, I would have to bring documentation of why. I would have to bring a doctor's note or write a letter to excuse my children for being absent. Sometimes they wouldn't accept a letter from me, I guess because it happened so often.

I finally decided to send Brittaney to live with her dad until she finished high school. She resented me for sending her to her dad, but I didn't know what else to do. She and her siblings were unruly, and I needed help. I know now that I made a mistake, and I should have kept her with me. I made a hasty decision and while I wish I could take it back, I can't.

I regret sending Brittaney and Maria away, but at the time I thought it was best for them and for me. They were so defiant, and I needed help. I know now that was not what they needed. If I could do it all over again, I would have kept them no matter what I did try to get them back, but they didn't want to be with me.

I made a lot of decisions that weren't the right decisions. In 2008, Denisha was skipping school and ran away. Her father sent her a ticket to Mississippi without my permission, and she went. I didn't know where she was for two weeks, and I was so afraid. All my children left me one by one.

When my son was 11 years old, I let him go see his dad in Mississippi and he didn't come back. His dad tricked me, and I felt like everyone knew that my son was not coming back including my daughters. I felt empty inside. I was devastated and crushed. I was lonely and sad. All my children were taken from me. I prayed, but I was angry with God. I wanted to know why he allowed my children to be taken from me.

I was ready to end it all by committing suicide. I ended up in the emergency room several times because I was so depressed. I ended up in counseling where I was diagnosed with anxiety and PTSD. I had a mental breakdown because I missed my children and wanted them to come back to me.

I ended up holding a grudge against my children and their fathers for many years. I turned my back on them because I felt that they abandoned me. There were times when I would visit them, but sometimes I couldn't visit them because I had no way to get there.

Losing my children didn't make money any easier, in fact, I ended up filing for bankruptcy. My wages were garnished, and I lost my apartment. I ended up finding a new apartment, but because of the bankruptcy payments; I didn't have enough to pay rent.

I would have to beg my children for money to pay my light bill and for gas to get to work. One of my daughters said I was doing crack, that's why I needed the money. When I heard I was devastated and didn't understand how my daughter could say such cruel things about me. Some of my children think I abandoned them and that I should have fought for them, but their fathers took them away from me.

One day when Denisha was around 20 years old something told me to go get her and bring her to Atlanta to visit me. It was God but I didn't know why. I drove to Mississippi to get Denisha and while she was with me, she complained that she had a headache. I thought it was a migraine, so I bought headache medication, but she kept complaining. I took her to the hospital, and they told her to take pain medication. While I was at work, she went back to the hospital again and they sent her home again. I saw thumping in her hair and head, she said, "if you leave me and go to work, I won't be here." I panicked and took off of work. I was scared I would get fired, but I didn't care. The doctor told us that Denisha had a brain tumor. Our mouths dropped! Denisha was afraid. She said, "I'm going to die, I'm going to die!" But even though I wasn't walking fully in faith, the Holy Spirit let me believe in the power of God's healing power. I prayed over her, declared the blood of Jesus, and prayed the Lord's prayer, just like I did for Maria. I kept praying as I walked the floor in her room. They sent her to another hospital for surgery. Her father, her daughter, my son, and her child's father were there, acting as if they had given up. They were making plans if she was already dead, but I refused to give up no matter what the report. I believed that the blood still works, and God is a healer! I was anxious, but I kept rebuking Satan and the spirit of death away from Denisha. I had to believe God for a miracle once again, as I did with Maria when she was hit by a car. Many people prayed for Denisha. There is power in prayer! The word says, where there are 2 or 3, God is amid it, and I believe that. Denisha survived but had to come back to Atlanta for another procedure. I was scared, but I had to have faith. They told us there was fluid leaking from her spine and back. I was terrified, and I prayed, "Lord, please help Denisha don't let her die."

I prayed that the blood of Jesus would heal her. I asked the Lord to heal Denisha's body and bless the doctors and the nurses. The procedure was painful for Denisha. I don't think they gave her pain medication before the procedure. When it was over, she was mad at me because I didn't speak up to her. I felt if they didn't stop the fluids that were leaking from her brain right away, she would have died. I was numb and scared, but I kept rebuking fear and the devil. I had to have faith and trust in the Lord. After the procedure, Denisha was okay. She still has headaches sometimes, but she survived. She is still alive! Thank you, Jesus!

The Bible says to forgive. For if you do not forgive man of their trespasses, God will not forgive you. I forgave so many including myself and I hope that my children forgive me. I am healing now so I choose forgiveness.

8

MOVING BACK HOME

In 2015, I left Atlanta and moved back to Cleveland for 2 years. After being in another abusive relationship. I met a man named Ricky, who I loved and thought loved me. He would wine and dine me. He told me how much he loved me. Two weeks later, he started trying to control me. My daughter came back at around the same time I met my boyfriend. I was so happy that one of my daughters finally came back to me. I wanted to spend time with my daughter, but he didn't want me to spend quality time with her.

I wanted to build a relationship with my daughter because I hadn't seen her in years, but he kept me with him at all times. He would isolate me from her by locking me in his apartment, so I couldn't get out without a key. He would come home and accuse me of leaving, but I told him I couldn't leave without the key. I didn't realize it at first, but he was on crack cocaine.

One day, he asked me if I was in love with him. I told him I was not in love with him, but I loved him. He shoved me away from him, and that was the first red flag. Another day, he pushed me and almost immediately apologized. One day, a friend called me, and he slapped me 5 times on my cheek when I got off the phone. He hit me so hard; that I saw stars. I did nothing at first, then I felt trapped, but I knew I had to defend myself. I started kicking and scratching him, and I dug my nails into his forehead to get him to leave me alone. There were so many red flags, and I finally took the way of escape and go back to my own apartment. I went back and forth with him, even though I knew he was no good for me.

When I was finally done with him, he started stalking me. He flattened 3 of my tires and I couldn't get to work. He would text me and call me names. He told me he was going to kill me. He took his truck and crashed it into my car. I filed a restraining order against him, and even though he was on the run, he was still harassing me. I had enough of being abused, and I wanted to be free.

In 2016, my boyfriend Ricky told me he changed, he got baptized and was in drug treatment programs. He was finally clean and sober. I thought this was God. I gave him the benefit of the doubt.

9

TAKING BACK WHAT'S MINE

In 2017, I moved to Minnesota with my boyfriend Ricky from Cleveland. When we got to Minnesota, he looked healthy and delivered, but two days later he started using crack again. I was devastated, and I was angry at myself for not going back to Cleveland. Ricky started treating me like a kid. He would make me sit and watch him do crack. I tried to run, but he would catch me before I could get away. When I escaped, he would call me, and I would run back to him. I was fed up with Ricky and his addiction to crack. I asked if he could do his drugs in another room, but he was determined to do them right in front of me.

He would ask me to drink even though he knew I was trying to stop drinking. It was hard not to give in when he kept offering it to me especially when I thought I needed a drink to deal with his psychotic/ schizophrenic behavior.

He would hallucinate and accuse me of trying to kill him. He said I had someone try to cut his neck off. He would holler as if someone was really cutting his neck off. Then he would peel the skin off his neck whenever he hallucinated about me having someone cut his neck off. One day, I got tired of him and tried to run, but he pinned me down in a chair so I couldn't leave. While he had me pinned down, he tried to have sex with me, but he was hallucinating again. He thought I was doing things and I wasn't. I was fed up. So, I went to a shelter for 1 month. He and his mother begged me to come back home. I gave him an ultimatum, I told him, "If you quit doing drugs, I will come back to you." He tricked me and told me that he would stop doing drugs completely, so I went back to him.

When he picked me up from the shelter, there was an immediate red flag that I ignored. His facial expressions said that he was not happy to see me and while I saw it, I dismissed it and went with him anyway. As soon as we got to Saint Paul, his demeanor changed. He started yelling at me and when he got out of the car, he slammed his phone on the ground. He kept hitting the car steering wheel. He yelled at me and said, "you want to go back!" I stayed calm to try to deescalate the situation, but he kept trying to agitate me. I wouldn't respond and he demanded that I say something. He said, "you act like you're slow." When we finally got home, he was distant like he had someone else.

The next night, he started doing crack again. I was furious, so I slapped the pipe out of his mouth. I wanted to beat him up, but I threw his glass pipe against the wall. That didn't stop him. He kept going back to get more crack until he got high. I lay on the couch, pissed off and ready to go back to the shelter. I would've gone too, but he had my EBT card and my car keys, so I couldn't go anywhere.

He came into the living room touching me and I could tell he was hallucinating. I told him to leave me alone, but he kept bothering me. I told him if he didn't leave me alone; I was going to call the police, and that" when things turned violent. He punched me in my head twice and I fell off the couch. He pulled me into the bedroom and punched me repeatedly in my eyes and my head. My eye was closed, and blood was gushing out from the trauma of him hitting me. I yelled his name over and over, then he stopped hitting me.

When I asked him to take me to the doctor, he said no with a smirk on his face as if he was enjoying me being in pain. I had to get out of there before he killed me. I told him I wanted a cigarette and when his back was turned, I called the police. The police arrived in about a minute, and I went to the battered women's shelter. I was traumatized and bitter. I couldn't believe that he told me to come to Minnesota and mistreat me. I hated him. I was in Minnesota all alone I didn't know nobody I didn't have no one to turn to. How could he treat me this way? I thought he loved me.

Despite how he treated me, I ended up marrying Ricky. We were only married three months before he went to prison, and I had to move into a shelter. He harassed me while he was in prison. He would tell me to come and get the divorce papers. We were only married for 3 months. I didn't understand why he married me and then wanted to divorce me. A year later, I found out he divorced me from another woman. When I confronted him about it, he said, "yeah bitch, we divorced," his voice was deep and nasty. When he called me a bitch, I told thanked him for doing all the paperwork for me. He moved on so fast. When I went to our apartment, another woman was living there. I banged on the demanding my important papers and car keys. The woman had a deep, raspy voice, and she told me they had a restraining order against me. When I got back to the shelter, Ricky's girlfriend called the shelter. I don't even know how they found out where I was staying, but she told me she was with Ricky, and I was numb.

I was devastated! She told me I needed to get my stuff from Ricky's case manager, but that never happened. Ricky kept all my stuff. The Lewis House shelter where I was staying, and my victim advocate sent someone to make a copy of my car key. I didn't get my things, but I got my car. He kept all my designer shoes, purses, and nice clothes. I didn't have any clothes, so the shelter gave me clothes to wear.

Sometime later someone stole my identity and I suspected it was Ricky. I left all my important documents at his house. I had to file a claim that my identity was stolen. I had to put a freeze on my credit reports to protect myself. I was so crushed and heartbroken that I began to question God. "Why did this happen to me? How can he sleep at night?"

I wanted revenge. I hated him but loved him too. He didn't contact me for 4 months. I was going crazy I didn't understand why. I wanted to hear his voice I couldn't sleep or eat right thinking about him. I wanted him to call me so bad. I was scared because I didn't know what he was doing. I thought he hated me, but I still wanted him. I didn't want to be alone with him again. I was traumatized and terrified of him but wanted to talk to him. If he told me to come around him, I wouldn't be able to because I was so scared of him finishing me off. I didn't understand why I wanted to talk to him, but I would not go around him. I wasn't healthy and this was not a healthy relationship. I needed help so I went to counseling to process my thoughts.

I cried at my therapy sessions. I was heartbroken, crushed, and devastated. There was no cure for a broken heart, it takes time to heal. I wanted to commit suicide because of the way he mistreated me. I was in so much pain and I wanted to pain to go away, but I decided I wasn't going to give up. Every time I felt sad, I would sing gospel songs in the shelter basement while doing my chores. When I would walk down the street, I would listen to songs to remind me that God is in control. I would sing so loud, and I would feel better.

As soon as I left the Lewis House, Ricky contacted me, but not because he cared. He wanted to harass me. I wrote a letter about the abuse I suffered, and Ricky stole the letter and attempted to harass me with it. Ricky dared to tell me, "Yeah I ain't do you like your uncles did you." Ricky told me what I wrote in the letter, and he told me he wanted me to commit suicide. I told him I didn't want to hear anymore. He kept saying, "I have your letter right here!" He was a sick narcissist with no empathy.

It all made sense to me. The reason he discarded me, beat me, cheated on me, and degraded me was that he found a fresh supply. Ricky had a couple of women the whole time we were together. The advocates at the shelter kept telling me to get a divorce. Whenever someone would tell me to divorce him, I would say that I wanted it to work, even though he beat me black and blue. Everybody thought I was stupid because I couldn't shake him. He had a stronghold on me. My friend Patricia told me it was because of soul ties. It took a couple of years for the soul ties to leave my spirit. I didn't want to divorce him. In the bible, it says in Malachi 2 verse 14, You ask, "Why are our gifts not accepted?" It is because the Lord saw the evil things you did—he is a witness against you. He saw you cheat on your wife. You have been married to her since you were young. She was your girlfriend. Then you made your vows to each other—and she became your wife." Verse 16 says, The Lord, the God of Israel, says, 'I hate divorce, and I hate the cruel things that men do. So, protect your spiritual unity. Don't cheat on your wife.'"

When I was taking classes about divorce, I learned that while God hates divorce; He hates sin more. Ricky broke our wedding vows when he beat me and cheated on me, so I was free to divorce him. I still couldn't get the nerve to divorce him, but I was thinking about it. While I was thinking about it, he divorced me without my knowledge. He acted like marriage was a piece of paper. I wasn't important to him. He didn't even fight for our marriage, and I was mad because he played with my heart and wasted my time. I felt so stupid, but I was relieved that it was over. Slowly but surely, I got over Ricky. If it wasn't for God, I don't think I could move on. God is so good! He's a burden bearer and a mind regulator. He was always there for me. The Lord helped ease the pain. I learned about forgiveness. I thought what Rick did to me was unforgivable until I read Matthew 18:21-22. It says, "Then Peter came to Him and said, 'Lord, how often shall my brother sin against me, and I forgive him? Up to seven times?' Jesus said to him, 'I do not say to you, up to seven times, but up to seventy times seven."

Although I said I forgive Ricky, I kept taking it back. It took me 3 years to forgive Ricky completely and put him in the Lord's hands. That's when I got serious about God - no more turning back and no more backsliding.

While I was at the shelter, I took classes and participated in Bible study every day. I am a witness that reading God's word will save you and deliver you from any situation that you are going through. I stayed in the women's shelter for 4 months. I stayed at the Lewis House in Minnesota. When my time was up at the Lewis House, I was devastated. I didn't want to go back to the same place, and I knew I still needed more help, so the staff referred me to The Dwelling Place. The Dwelling Place was a Christian-based shelter program. This is where I gave my life to the lord. I didn't want to go to another shelter, but I needed more help.

Although I stayed in a shelter with my kids it was only for a month. Now I was going from shelter to shelter and while I was grateful to have somewhere to live. I didn't like living with strangers, so I was uncomfortable. I always had my own place.

I was grateful for the shelters because I could have been living in my car homeless, broke with no money, and no food. But God! He had a plan for my life. The Lord sent me to these shelters so that I could learn about Him. I was so grateful, and I thank God for everything they did for me.

It was bittersweet living at The Dwelling Place. I was happy most of the time and I felt safe. We had several classes that I benefited from. My favorite classes at the shelter were all about getting me from where I was to where God wanted me to be. Some of the teachers and staff were very supportive and taught me well. I got stronger, and I learned that I have been in abusive relationships all my life. The staff made sure that we went to church every Sunday, and it helped me get through the week and eased some of the pain.

I had many challenges living in The Dwelling Place. My roommate was Muslim, and I was a Christian. She would get offended because I would worship our room. She would put her phone in the sitting area before dawn in the morning to play music and chant.

I would wake up and hear loud chanting and music playing. She was playing loud music while I slept, and I was angry at her. I would turn her phone off without her permission. She would come running into the room and take her phone from me. I asked her to stop playing that music in the living room. She put her phone in there a couple more days after, then she stopped. She would blurt out Allah is God, then she would mock Jesus by playing a video on her phone. The video said that Jesus was a prophet, and he wasn't crucified. The video also said that Mohammad wrote the Quran.

We didn't get along because of our different beliefs in religion. She stopped speaking to me for about 2 months and that was OK with me. I wanted to set a boundary with her. She had bad boundaries and I had no other option but to report her to the staff.

The Dwelling Place is a Christian organization for battered women and children. Some of the caseworkers told me to love my roommate, but they didn't help me with my roommate.

When I lived at The Dwelling Place, my caseworker told me I needed to get a job. I needed more time to get on my feet, but my case worker was insistent. I tried to explain that I was sick because of surgery. I was also depressed, disabled, and unable to work like I used to.

So, I moved to Naomi's Shelter in Saint Paul. Naomi's Place was a better fit for me because they didn't force me to get a job right away. They wanted me to learn about God and heal. While I lived at Naomi's place, I had my own bathroom, and it was like my own apartment. I learned so much in the classes I attended at Naomi. I stayed there for about 10 months. The staff wanted me to stay longer but my caseworker found me an apartment.

I was so excited about being on my own again in my new, affordable apartment. God set me free using the classes I took and the counseling I received at the shelters. I also took part in my healing by reading God's word, praying, going to church, forgiving those that offended me, and forgiving myself. Just like a butterfly is a caterpillar before it becomes a butterfly. When I think about the transformation a caterpillar goes through before it becomes a butterfly, I can understand my transformation. I'm not the same. I don't look like what I went through. I changed and I'm growing. The healing process began with setting goals, resting in God, and putting God first. Now, I'm in my place. I haven't been in a relationship for 3 years. I'm not having sex. I go to church every week. I'm a PCA. I am FREE from domestic violence. I recognize red flags. My boundaries are healthy. I know my worth. I'm filled with the Holy Ghost. I'm saved and sanctified by the blood of the Lamb.

God Beauty for My Ashes. God is keeping me. I'm FREE!

EPILOGUE

If you are reading this book, and you are in a domestic violence relationship with anyone. Domestic violence can happen to men, women, boys, and girls. Domestic violence happens in all races, cultures, and backgrounds. Recognize the red flags and don't ignore the first red flag. It's there. When you see the red flag, get out safely. Don't panic, wait until you are safe and have a bag already packed with your important papers, etc. If you are a victim of domestic violence, you can be set FREE. God is a deliverer and a healer. There is help out there to reach out for help by calling the domestic violence hotline, but choose a good shelter where the word is taught, and you feel comfortable. May God bless all those who are struggling with domestic issues or trauma. In The Name of Jesus Christ of Nazareth, Amen!

About the Author

Denise Davis is a survivor of childhood and adult trauma. Originally from Cleveland, Ohio, Denise has overcome a great deal of trauma and pain. She is the mother of 5 children. She enjoys going to church, singing and listening to gospel music. Denise also loves to swim, skate, crochet and play games.